I WANT TO PLAY WITH THE SUN

Story by Rick Bergh
Music by Erica Phare-Bergh
Artwork by Franceska Dnestrianschii

I Want to Play with the Sun
Copyright © 2015 by R.E.Bergh Consulting Inc.

Find the *5-BIG Words*:
amazed | tuque | confused | blame | hurled

**For the FREE sing-a-long song and FREE *5-BIG Words* learning page, please go
to www.asongwitheverystory.com/iwanttoplaywiththesun/**

Also available online for purchase is a <u>Music Educator's Package</u> that includes:
♫ **Original song back-up track**
♫ **Song chart**
♫ **Classical composer worksheet (excerpt hidden within each song)**
♫ **Lesson plan**

Go to: **www.asongwitheverystory.com/iwanttoplaywiththesun/teacher/**

Published by   **BEACON MOUNT**
‒‒‒‒ **P U B L I S H I N G** ‒‒‒‒

18 West Chapman Place, Cochrane, Alberta, T4C 1J9, Canada.
www.asongwitheverystory.com

ISBN 978-0-9947962-3-3 (Paperback)
ISBN 978-1-988082-14-1 (Hardcover)
ISBN 978-0-9947962-4-0 (ePub)
ISBN 978-1-988082-11-0 (Mobi)

Printed in the United States of America

Dedicated to my firstborn, Devon,
who was the inspiration behind this story
and asked to play with the sun
when he was a young boy.

One day, Devon and his dad drove down the gravel road in their little red car. Devon looked up at the sky and said, "Dad, I want to play with the sun!" "You can't play with the sun," his father replied. "Why not?" Devon asked and he reached up and pulled the sun out of the sky.

His father was amazed. Devon could hardly wait to go home and play with the sun in his backyard.

7

When they got home, Devon jumped out of the car, with the sun in his hands.

"Look, Mom!" he shouted. "Look what I have!" "What's that?" Devon's mother asked.

"Can't you feel the warmth? It's the sun!" he replied. "How did you get the sun?" she asked. "I just reached up in the sky and grabbed it," Devon said proudly.

"Dad, let's play catch," Devon said. So Devon and his dad threw the sun back and forth. It was fun to play with the sun.

"Mom, let's play soccer," Devon said.
"Okay," his mother replied. So they took off their shoes and
kicked the sun with their bare feet.
It was fun to play with the sun.

11

A little later, Devon's best friend, Nathan, came over to play. He was wearing his winter coat, his gloves, his scarf, his boots and his bright red tuque.
"Nathan!" Devon said, "Why are you wearing your winter clothes?"
"Because it's so cold out!" Nathan replied.

"It's not cold here in the backyard," Devon said. "Hey! You're right!" Nathan agreed. "I think I'll put my shorts back on." So Nathan went home, but he never came back to play.

It was lunchtime and Devon ran into the house.
He looked out the front window.
"Why is it so dark out?" he asked his mother. "It's only noon."
"It's dark because you've taken the sun," she replied.

"You should put it back in the sky for everyone to enjoy," she continued.
"No way!" Devon said, "It's MY sun and I'm going to keep it!"
"Are you sure that's the right thing to do, Devon?" his mother asked.

Devon's entire town was mixed up that afternoon.
It was so dark that neighbors were bumping into each other, cars were
crashing, and everyone was confused.

The policewoman was going from house to house looking for the sun.
"Have you seen the sun?" she would ask. "No!" each person replied.
"No, I haven't!"

Then the policewoman drove to Devon's house. "Hello," she said to Devon's father. "Hello, officer. May I help you?" he asked.

"Maybe," the policewoman said, "We're looking for the sun. It seems that someone has stolen it from the sky," she said.

Devon heard the policewoman talking and ran to the front door to listen.

Just as she was about to leave, Devon spoke up bravely,
"Officer, what is *stealing*?"
"Well, Devon," the policewoman said, "it's when you
take something that doesn't belong to you."
"Is the sun mine?" Devon asked.
"Yes, the sun is yours, but it also belongs to everyone."

"But the sun is mine too, right?" he asked again.
"Yes, it is," the policewoman replied. "Then, *I do* have the sun! It's in my sandbox," Devon said. She looked at Devon and said, "Hm. You have an important decision to make, young man." Then she turned and walked away.

"Mom, do you want to kick the sun arround with me?"
Devon asked. "No thanks, Devon," his mother said.

Devon thought to himself, "I'm going to phone up Nathan, my best friend.
He'll play with me for sure!"
But even Nathan didn't want to play with Devon because he heard that Devon
had the sun and wasn't sharing it.

23

Devon sat on the grass in the middle of his backyard.
He realized that he was all alone.
Nobody wanted to play with him anymore.
So he walked into town and left the sun behind.

People were still upset. They continued to blame each other for stealing the sun. It was no longer a happy town.

Devon ran back to his sandbox and picked up the sun.

"This sun is for everyone, not just for me," he said to himself.
"I want people to be happy. And I want my friends back."

And so with all his strength, Devon hurled the sun back into the sky.

Instantly, the whole town changed. People stopped arguing and fighting. Instead, they began to smile and laugh. They put on their shorts and T-shirts and drank ice-cold lemonade.

28

And then came Nathan. He was running across the street wearing his blue shorts, his green T-shirt, his white running shoes... and his bright red tuque.

29

I Want to Play with the Sun
Words and music by Erica Phare-Bergh

Chorus:
I want to play with the sun - yeah, yeah, yeah
I want to share it with everyone - yeah
I want to play with the sun - yeah, yeah, yeah
And share its warmth with you

When I get something special
I share it with a friend
Instead of holding onto it
It's more fun in the end

Chorus:

Every day's much better
When people learn to share
Show your friends you love them
And that you really care

Excerpt: Gioachino Rossini's *William Tell Overture:* "Call to the Cows"

Chorus:

Also available in the *A Song with Every Story* series

Mr.Lumberjack

Mr.Lumberjack is horrified when he discovers his forest in a shambles. A journey takes him to the culprit and a surprise ending leads to a valuable lesson.

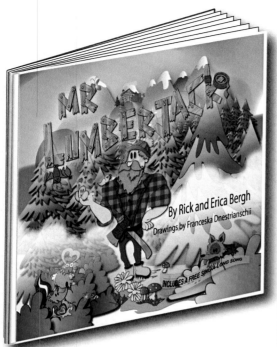

The Stretchy Cheese Pizza

Connor's mom invites him to make his very own pizza, but he soon discovers that the mound of cheese that he put on top has a mind of its own....

I Want to Grow a Beard

Connor wants to grow up too quickly and be just like his dad. His dream comes true the next morning when he wakes up with a full beard. But he soon discovers that being an adult isn't all that it's cracked up to be.

Please check out our books at *www.asongwitheverystory.com*

Made in the USA
Middletown, DE
21 November 2015